Weather Watch!

THE WEATHER
IN
WINTER

Miriam Moss

Wayland

Weather Watch!

Other titles in this series include:
The Weather in Spring
The Weather in Summer
The Weather in Autumn

Cover pictures: Images of winter – (main picture) Red berries on a holly bush. (top left) Two Emperor penguins on Ross Island, Antarctica. (centre)The beautiful patterns created by ice crystals. (bottom right) Winter frost on oak leaves.

Contents page: This field is covered completely in deep snow in winter.

Editor: Deb Elliott
Designer: Malcolm Walker

Text is based on *Winter Weather* in the *Seasonal Weather* series published in 1990.

First published in 1994 by
Wayland (Publishers) Ltd
61 Western Road, Hove
East Sussex, BN3 1 JD, England

British Library Cataloguing in Publication Data
Moss, Miriam
  Weather in Winter. - (Weather Watch! Series)
  I. Title II. Series
  551.6

ISBN 0-7502-1185-7
Typeset by Kudos
Printed and bound by Casterman S.A., Belgium

CONTENTS

KEEPING WARM 4
WINTER SUNSHINE 6
DEEP SNOW AND FROZEN RAIN 8
WINTER WINDS 10
ALL SORTS OF CLOUDS 12
SNOW, FOG AND FROST 14
POLAR WINTER 16
ALL KINDS OF WINTERS 18
DANGEROUS WEATHER 20
COLD AND WARM SEAS 22
ICE FOR AGES 24
WEATHER WATCHERS 26
MEASURING TEMPERATURE 28
GLOSSARY 30
BOOKS TO READ 31
INDEX 32

KEEPING WARM

⬆ *Why do you think the woods in winter often seem so silent and still?*

What does winter mean to you? Does it mean keeping warm by wrapping up in thick coats, scarves, hats and gloves? Perhaps winter makes you think of bare trees and frost on the windows. Winter for some people means fierce snowstorms. Other people in the world have warm winters. They never see ice or snow at all!

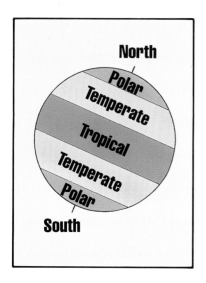

← *Different parts of the world have different kinds of weather. In tropical countries the weather is almost always warm. In temperate countries the weather changes four times in each year. These changes are called seasons. At the North and South Poles it is always very cold, especially in winter.*

↓ *Did you know that you lose most of your body heat from your head? Wearing a hat keeps you warm in cold weather!*

Can you see the Sun shining through the branches of this tree? The Sun is low in the sky and the Sun's rays are weaker in winter. ➡

⬇ *As the Earth spins, the countries tilted towards the Sun have the warmer weather.*

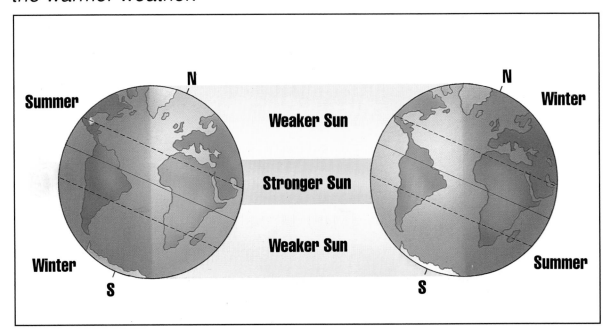

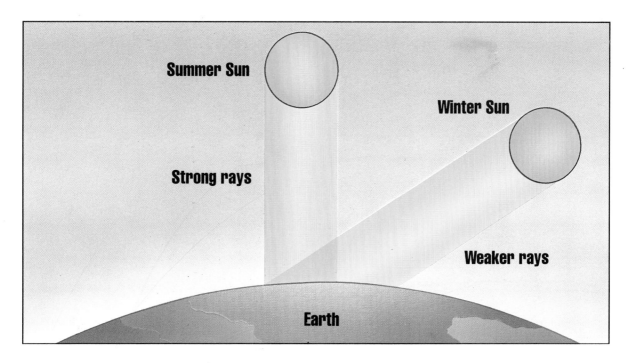

⬆ *In winter the Sun's rays have further to travel and so they are weaker.*

The four changes in the weather are called seasons. They are summer, autumn, winter and spring.

When the country you live in is tilted towards the Sun, you have the hottest weather and it is summer. When your part of the world tilts away from the Sun, you have cooler weather and it is winter.

Trapping heat

Clouds trap heat. They act just like a blanket or duvet and stop heat escaping. Can you think of some other ways that we trap in heat to keep warm in winter?

↑   *In winter, it gets dark earlier. This is because the nights are longer and there are fewer hours of daylight. As winter sets in, the land and the sea become cooler. When they have lost all their summer's warmth, the cold weather really begins.*

Hailstones are not stones at all but lumps of frozen raindrops. ➡

⬇ Icy winds blow in winter. In the mornings windows, pavements and trees are covered in frost. The rain freezes and falls as snow. During the long winter nights, fog and mist lie in the valleys. Often the weak winter Sun cannot drive away the fog.

← *A bitterly cold wind blows over the Himalayan Mountains in winter.*

Winds from hot lands bring warm air with them. Some winds blow at the same time in the same place every year. These winds have special names which are on the two diagrams on the right. ➜

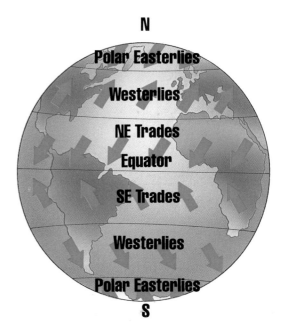

N

Polar Easterlies

Westerlies

NE Trades

Equator

SE Trades

Westerlies

Polar Easterlies

S

The main winds on Earth

The air around us rises up when it is hot and sinks down when it is cold. Heat from the Sun makes the air lighter and rise up. Cooler air from somewhere else rushes into the space left. Do you know what this rushing air is? It's the wind!

The wind blows the leaves off the trees in autumn. It makes clothes flap about and turns umbrellas inside out. All over the world warm and cold winds blow. Bitterly cold winds come from the frozen lands at the North and South Poles.

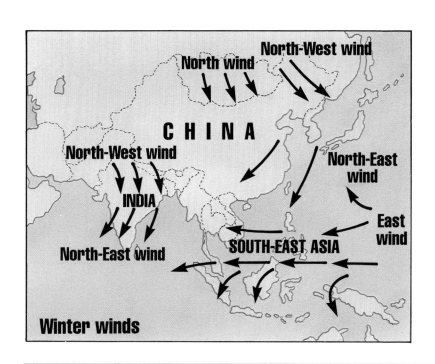

ALL SORTS OF CLOUDS

Have you ever wondered what clouds are made of? They are made of tiny droplets of water. When the Sun heats the sea, tiny droplets of water are carried up into the air. When they are high enough, they cool and join together and can be seen as fluffy white clouds in the sky. Then the wind blows the clouds about - through warm or cool air. When they pass through cool air the droplets get bigger and heavier until they fall as rain.

↓ *How clouds are made.*

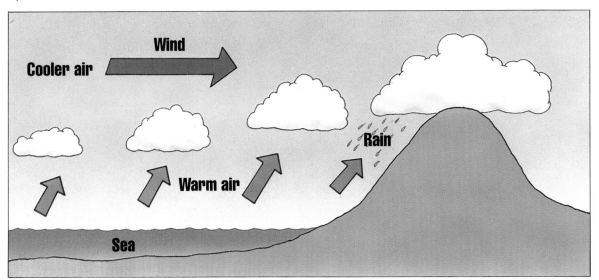

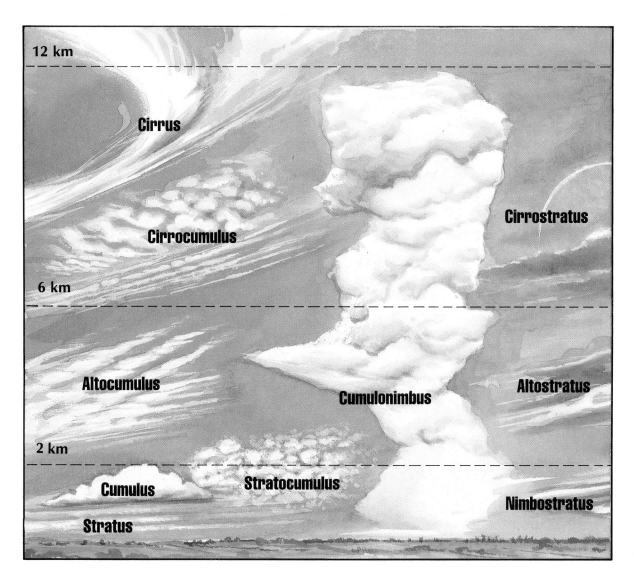

12 km

Cirrus

Cirrocumulus

Cirrostratus

6 km

Altocumulus

Cumulonimbus

Altostratus

2 km

Cumulus

Stratocumulus

Nimbostratus

Stratus

↑ *Look how many different sorts of clouds there are. Can you see any of these clouds in the sky today?*

SNOW, FOG AND FROST

If the air below a cloud is very cold, the water droplets freeze and fall as snow instead of rain. ➡

Cold air
SNOW

Warm air
RAIN

⬇ The snow clouds have passed over leaving a blanket of snow and a clear blue sky.

↑ *Thick fog lying in a deep valley in winter.*

Walking through fog is like walking through a cloud. Do you know why we have fog? When warm water droplets in the air settle on cold ground, they turn into mist or fog. In winter, water droplets in the air sometimes settle on very cold ground and freeze into ice crystals.

POLAR WINTER

The coldest places on Earth are the North and South Poles. Winter here can last for nearly nine months of the year! At the North Pole the Sun sets in September and is not seen again until the end of March. Then it is dark all through the day as well as all night!

↓ *These Inuit children who live in the frozen north of Canada wrap up well against the bitter winter weather.*

⬆ *Huge icebergs at the South Pole rise out of the frozen sea like strange monsters.*

Without sunshine at the Poles the seas grow colder and colder. By August the edges of the sea begin to freeze. Then the heavy winter storms begin. Freezing winds roar across the icy land and the snow is whipped up into blinding blizzards.

Did you know?

The coldest place in the world is the South Pole where the temperature can fall to -89 °C (-128 °F).

There many different kinds of winters on Earth. One reason for this is that land cools down more quickly than the sea. So, in winter the sea stays warmer for longer. This means that places a long way from the sea, in the middle of a large area of land, have much colder winters than places by the sea.

↑ *Snow settles in an American canyon.*

Another reason for the different winters are the cold and warm winter winds. Lands which have warm winds from the tropics blowing across them in winter have mild winters. Other countries have freezing winds from the North and South Poles, making their winters bitterly cold.

↑ *Winter skiers in Australia.*

Winters are very cold in the Russian capital, Moscow, which is a long way from the sea. ➡

⬇ *These Swedish children ski to school in winter.*

DANGEROUS WEATHER

Many people think that snow only falls in cold countries. Did you know that snow also falls in hot lands? Snow falls in Africa, Saudi Arabia and sometimes, when there is a very hard winter, in the desert.

↓ *A cactus covered in snow in the Arizona desert, USA*

Question: When does the sea stop moving?

Answer: When it freezes solid! (See picture on page 21.)

Cars get stuck in the deep snow after a very heavy snowstorm and roads become blocked. If the snow melts and then freezes again in the night, the road turns into a sheet of ice, making travelling very dangerous. ➜

↓ *The sea stood still! It froze over completely in England in 1963.*

↑ *A warm current, called the Gulf Stream, flows around Norway in winter. It keeps the seas ice-free during the cold winters.*

Did you know that the oceans around the land change the kind of winter weather we have? Sometimes the sea that flows past in winter is warm because it has travelled from a warmer part of the world.

⬇ *In winter, cold ocean currents sweep down from the North Pole to Canada. They freeze this river even though it is much further south than Norway and nearer to warmer countries.*

ICE FOR AGES

↓ *This glacier is high up in the mountains in New Zealand.*

The weather on Earth has not always been like it is now. Thousands of years ago, all of Europe was covered in deep snow and glaciers. Glaciers are rivers of ice. They travel downhill so slowly that you cannot see them moving!

↓ *A few hundred years ago there were some unusually cold winters. During these winters, the River Thames in London froze over completely. Frost fairs were held on the ice. What kinds of things are going on at this frost fair in 1814?*

WEATHER WATCHERS

Did you know that we can tell what the weather will be like tomorrow or next week? Information about the weather is collected all over the world by scientists.
They collect it from satellites spinning high in space, from ships at sea and from local weather stations.
The information is fed into computers which print out the weather for the days ahead on weather maps.

⬇ *Weather balloons sent high into the air tell scientists what the weather will be like.*

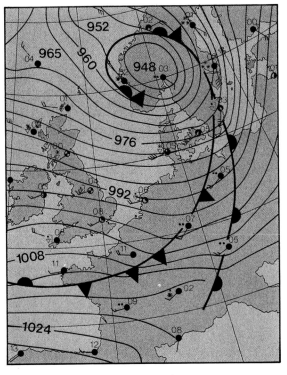

↑ *A simple weather map*

↑ *Satellite picture*

← *Key*

Weather symbols

✱	Snow	● ▽	Rain showers
● ✱	Sleet	✱ ▽	Snow showers
△ ▽	Hail showers	✎	Cloud cover (full cover)
● ●	Light rain	✓	Wind speed and direction
● ●	Moderate rain		

Find the weather symbols on the key for snow and rain. Now look at the weather map. What kind of weather is there over Great Britain?

Have you ever been ill and had your temperature taken using a thermometer?
A thermometer measures how much heat is being given off by something.

↓ *This man is measuring changes in the temperature of the air outside.*

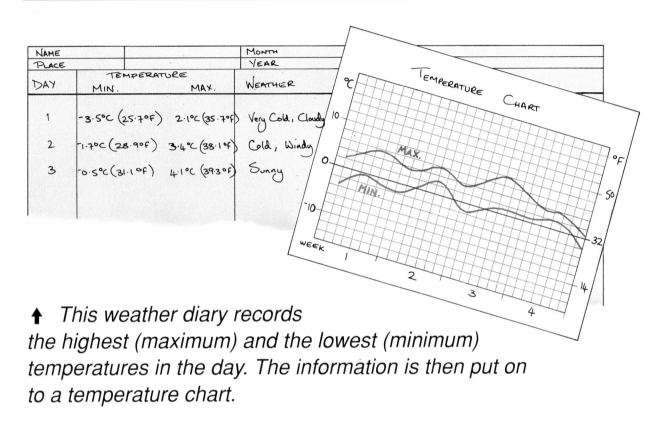

NAME			MONTH	
PLACE			YEAR	
DAY	TEMPERATURE		WEATHER	
	MIN.	MAX.		
1	-3.5°C (25.7°F)	2.1°C (35.7°F)	Very Cold, Cloudy	
2	-1.7°C (28.9°F)	3.4°C (38.1°F)	Cold, Windy	
3	-0.5°C (31.1°F)	4.1°C (39.3°F)	Sunny	

↑ *This weather diary records*
the highest (maximum) and the lowest (minimum)
temperatures in the day. The information is then put on
to a temperature chart.

Weather watchers measure the temperature of the air around us each day using two thermometers. One measures the highest temperature of the air and one measures the lowest temperature.

Do you know how thermometers work? They have thin glass tubes inside them filled with liquid. When the liquid gets warmer it rises up the tube. The temperature is read off a scale at the side.

GLOSSARY

blizzard A winter storm with strong winds and heavy snow.

cactus A plant with a swollen stem and spines, which grows in hot, dry deserts.

canyon A very deep valley often cut by a river.

ice crystals Tiny regular shapes of ice.

frost A thin layer of tiny ice crystals.

glacier A slow-moving mass of ice and snow.

hail Pieces of ice which sometimes form in high clouds.

ocean current A moving flow of water in the oceans.

ray A narrow beam of light.

satellite A spacecraft which circles high above the Earth. Some satellites send back information about the weather.

temperature An exact measure of how hot or cold something is.

Books to read

Glaciers and Ice Caps by Martyn Bramwell
  (Franklin Watts, 1986)
Let's Celebrate Winter by Rhoda Nottridge
  (Wayland, 1994)
Projects For Winter by Celia McInnes (Wayland, 1988)
Snowy Weather by Jillian Powell (Wayland, 1992)
Weather and Climate by Judy Langthorne and Gaye
  Conroy (Wayland, 1992)
Windy Weather by Jillian Powell (Wayland, 1992)
Winter Weather by John Mason (Wayland, 1990)

Picture acknowledgements
The publishers would like to thank the following for allowing their pictures to be reproduced in this book: Bryan and Cherry Alexander 16, 21 (top); David Bowden Photo Library 18 (bottom); Cephas Picture Library 18 (top); Bruce Coleman Ltd cover main (Adrian Davies), 4, 20; Dundee Meterological Office 27; ET Archive 25; Chris Fairclough Colour Library 6, 19 (both); Geoscience Features 8, 15, 21 (bottom), 22; Eric and David Hosking 9 (top); The Hutchison Library 5; Oxford Scientific Films 17; Tony Stone Worldwide cover top (Roger Mear), cover centre, cover bottom (Geoff Johnson), 14, 23, 24; Wayland Picture Library 10 (Jimmy Holmes), 28 (Paul Seheult); Zefa contents page, 9 (bottom), 26. All illustrations by Peter Bull Art except for those on pages 27 and 29 which are by the Hayward Art Group.

INDEX

Australia 18

Canada 16, 23
clouds 7, 12-13

fog 15
frost 9
  fairs 25

glaciers 24-5

hailstones 9

ice 4, 21, 24-5
  crystals 15

keeping warm 4-5, 7

New Zealand 25

Poles, the 5, 11, 16-17, 18, 23

rain 9, 12

seas 22-3
seasons 5, 7
skiing 18, 19
snowstorms 4, 14, 17, 21
sunshine 6, 7

temperate countries 5
tropical countries 5, 18

winds 9, 10-11, 17
weather stations 26
weather watchers 26-7, 29